*a garden
from a
hundred
packets of
seed*

illustrations by kate gibb

james fenton

a garden from a hundred packets of seed

VIKING
an imprint of
PENGUIN BOOKS

VIKING

Published by the Penguin Group
Penguin Books Ltd, 80 Strand, London WC2R 0RL, England
Penguin Putnam Inc., 375 Hudson Street, New York, New York 10014, USA
Penguin Books Australia Ltd, Ringwood, Victoria, Australia
Penguin Books Canada Ltd, 10 Alcorn Avenue, Toronto, Ontario, Canada M4V 3B2
Penguin Books India (P) Ltd, 11 Community Centre,
Panchsheel Park, New Delhi – 110 017, India
Penguin Books (NZ) Ltd, Cnr Rosedale and Airborne Roads,
Albany, Auckland, New Zealand
Penguin Books (South Africa) (Pty) Ltd, 24 Sturdee Ave,
Rosebank 2196, South Africa

Penguin Books Ltd, Registered Offices: 80 Strand, London WC2R 0RL, England

www.penguin.com

First published 2001
2

Copyright © James Fenton, 2001
Illustrations copyright © Kate Gibb, 2001
The moral right of the author has been asserted

Set in Trump Medieval
Typeset by Rowland Phototypesetting Ltd, Bury St Edmunds, Suffolk
Printed in Great Britain by The Bath Press

A CIP catalogue record for this book is available from the British Library

ISBN 0-670-91108-9

To Michael Collins,
without whom there would be no garden

This book is based on a series of articles
which first appeared in the *Guardian*. My thanks to
Annalena McAfee and Alice Munsey.

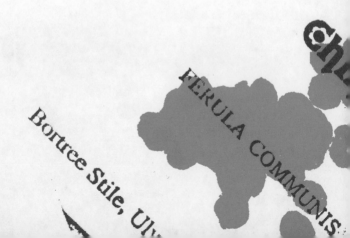

Bortree Stile, Ulv   FERULA COMMUNIS

contents

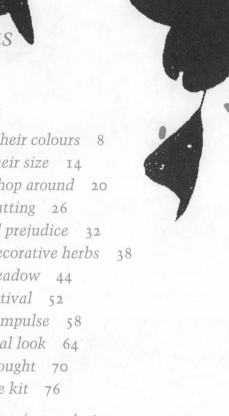

Seeds

introduction

Of course you may say it is only a game, and indeed
it *is* a game: a game of lists. What plants would you
choose to grow, given a blank slate of a garden, and
given the stipulation that everything you grow in this
garden must be raised by you from seed? It is a game
of choice, but it could be more than a game. At the
very least, it could be a way of thinking afresh about
how to put a garden together, and with what purpose
in mind.

For years now the gardening press (newspaper
columns, magazines and glossy books) has been,
consciously and unconsciously, campaigning for a
common approach. One starts with a design, the
'bones' of the garden, the 'structure'. Next one shades
in plausible areas and shapes, indicating trees, shrubs
and perennials. Finally one is supposed to go out and
buy the plants pencilled in in those plausible shapes.
The rest is mostly maintenance.

This approach to gardening would never have
become plausible or popular if it did not reflect a
certain wisdom. But may I respectfully suggest that it
is not the only way to garden? It may be one wise way

to operate, but it is not the only wisdom available to human kind. To take the simplest counter-example: an allotment gardener does not have to start with a design. The important question is: what do I want to grow?

The design of an allotment is hardly an issue. Content is everything. So the allotment gardener in January may be happily and appropriately engaged in the simple act of compiling lists: this is what I want to eat this year, or this is what I want to grow for the challenge, or this is what has piqued my curiosity.

Why should the flower gardener not feel the same? Why should he or she not ask: what do I feel like growing this year? What delights me? What bores me? What is ravishing? What is revolting? Flower fanatic and vegetable fiend, we are seated at the same kitchen table, leafing through many of the same catalogues. The same gales are howling around the rooftops. The same frosts are glazing the water-butts. Why should I not feel, this January, the same freedom as my pea-epicurean, my marrow-maniacal friend?

The first answer that springs to mind is that a flower garden is of its nature a permanent thing, whereas an allotment, to all intents and purposes, closes down for the winter. But this objection need not necessarily hold. After all, I have not yet defined the sort of flower garden I am thinking of. Indeed, I do not want to define it at all too nicely, because I am ambitious to hold the attention of more than one kind of reader (including, of course, the allotment gardener).

So my definition – my non-definition – of a garden must include a spectacular one that I saw last summer in Manhattan, which consisted of nothing but morning glories grown on a fire-escape, high up above the street. Mustard and cress sown on a face-flannel, Virginia stock in an old crab-shell, or a row of hyacinths in their glasses – all these count as gardens, in my understanding of the word, along with Great Dixter, Powis Castle and Versailles.

For those who have landed on some property of which they can say, 'This is where I hope to live for the next so-many years,' I have some advice, which may prove welcome, since it may well prove cheap. It is *not* the case that your permanent plantings, your graph-paper layout of shrubs and perennials (supposing this to be your ultimate goal), should be put in place as soon as possible. If you are renovating an old garden, or starting one from scratch, it may well be good practice to plant experimentally for a couple of seasons, relying mainly on annuals, until the soil has been well conditioned and the perennial weeds have been largely defeated.

The larger the garden, the more welcome this practice will be. Your shrubs and your perennials may take time to bulk up, whereas your annuals are by definition going to perform in one season. But that is not the end of the story. Many annuals will make a

permanent contribution to the garden by seeding
themselves around. The smaller ones may find their
way into nooks and crannies where it would have
been hard to plant them in the first place. The larger
ones may, if given a chance, make impressive
colonies, in the way that opium poppies do. So they
will come back in profusion year after year.

But of course not every would-be gardener has the
prospect of owning or occupying the same plot of
ground for a large number of years. One moves
on. One moves up in the world. One moves
down in the world. One comes home and
finds the locks changed and one's luggage
on the street. Not everyone wants to
lavish the same expenditure on a small
garden as on a small kitchen (although
it is amazing how often the designers
of small gardens will work on this
assumption, allowing a budget of
£12,000 to put in that 'bone-structure').

This list is not only about annuals.
It looks at any sort of plant that
can be appropriately grown from
seed. I do not propose that you
start your roses in this way:
that would be, as Peter Pan
says of death, an awfully *big*
adventure. But I aim to
devise a diverse and

interesting starter kit for a garden, balancing the obvious (but irresistible) with the more recherché.

As for the design of this flower garden, I insist on keeping it vague. A hundred varieties of flower might look cramped on a balcony, spectacular in a situation only one size up from there. For it is amazing what can be crammed into a small space. Conversely, it is amazing the number of plants that could, in theory, be raised from so large a number as a hundred packets of seed.

I think that the proposed garden should, on the whole, be fairly sunny; and perhaps it should have some soil. But if the soil is an utter write-off, there is time (imagining still that this is read in January) to think of railway sleepers and raised beds. In my previous garden, I struggled with clay and builders' rubble. One day a friend, an expert gardener, came to see my efforts. They were pitiable. My friend told me to buy railway sleepers, put weedkiller on what I had so far, and build raised beds, importing the soil for them and making no attempt to reform the soil I had.

I listened to what he was telling me in some dismay, and I ignored his advice. But I remembered it all the second time around, when I moved to a derelict farm and proceeded to lay out a garden on all kinds of not entirely promising terrain. I no longer believed that subsoil would, in the course of a few seasons, magically transform itself into topsoil. Where soil was needed, we imported it, along with manure, grit, sand and mushroom compost: piles and piles of the stuff have been required over the years, but that is because we have been working on an ambitious scale.

But even with an average town garden, if you have to import soil, buy it in bulk, rather than by the bag. It is depressing how many bags you would need to fill a modest raised bed, and it is astonishing how much can be spent during a quick impatient trip to a garden centre. Conversely, it is gratifying to see how costs can be reduced by sensible bulk buying.

But this is not a book about huge projects. It is about thinking your way towards an essential flower garden, by the most traditional of routes: planting some seeds and seeing how they grow. And the seeds I have chosen are, generally speaking, ones which have, over several years, given me pleasure in my garden. This is my personal anthology.

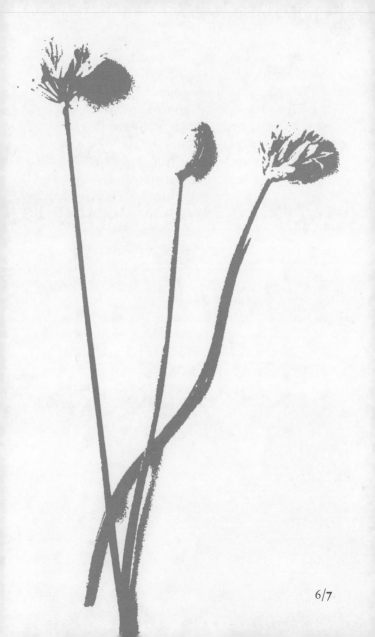

*flowers
and
their
colours*

[6)

First and foremost, flowers attract us by their colours. But of course it is not us they are trying so hard to attract: it is the birds, the butterflies, the insects, and those legendary night-pollinating moths. If a flower garden gives me the impression that it is flowering there for my pleasure and benefit, it is engaged in a deception. And if I fall for that deception, I am like someone who, entering a crowded room, believes that all eyes are upon him, when in fact all eyes are upon the swarm of bees visible just over his shoulder.

'How beautiful are the retired flowers!' wrote Keats in a famous passage; 'how they would lose their beauty were they to throng into the highway crying out, "admire me I am a violet! dote upon me I am a primrose!"' In fact that is exactly what the flowers, even the retired flowers, are saying to their pollinators. Or if not that, then they are saying something coarser.

And their colours, which provoke in us such a profound and complex response, were once their exclusive property. No one saw such colours, unless it was in a flower, or a gemstone, or some extraordinary artifice such as purple-dyed cloth. Some flowers may have disturbed or repelled by their mysterious or obscene shapes, but none, surely, were thought ugly for their colours. Sad, perhaps. But never ugly.

Today some makers of gardens are so browbeaten by colour-snobbery that they settle for a garden in which all flowers are excluded, or they take nervous care to check which flowers, which colours, are okay. Gardening writers, in the hope of giving the weight of science to their reflections, talk about combinations of complementary colours, and sometimes even refer to the colour-wheel. But this is uncandid taste masquerading as high theory.

There is no point in asking, in the abstract, whether burnt orange will look well alongside vermilion. A garden is not a canvas, and even with a canvas the question has no answer. How large a patch of burnt orange, in relation to how large a patch of vermilion – and what else is going on within the proposed colour field? Is the gardener who thinks of placing a burnt orange flower beside a vermilion one taking into account the colour and relative importance of the leaves? Or is it assumed that all greens are somehow factored out by the retina?

Gardening is quite unlike painting, but there are things one can learn from the painter nevertheless. John Gage, the great historian of colour theory, tells a story of Turner and Constable exhibiting their paintings side by side in 1832 in the crowded conditions of Somerset House. Painters in these exhibitions (and Turner in particular) specialized in

flowers and their colours

last-minute tricks to ensure that their works looked well.

On this occasion Constable found 'the red robes of the dignitaries in his picture of the *Opening of Waterloo Bridge* (London, National Gallery) cast into obscurity by the wafer of red sealing-wax which Turner applied to the water of his cool green sea-piece next to it, *Helvoetsluys*, and later painted into the form of a buoy. "He has been here," said Constable when he saw it, "and fired a gun."'

Some small flowers possess this ability to 'fire a gun'. #1,* pheasant's eye, the hardy annual *Adonis aestivalis*, is a flower with the force of a concentrated blood-red anemone – a small ranunculus in other words. The kind of flower you would expect to find in a Mughal miniature, or in the border of a Book of Hours. You give it a place to grow. It comes back year after year, an unerring shot.

And in such company who could object to the classic #2, cornflower, *Centaurea cyanus*, a flower more often seen in the shops these days than ever before. The gardener should not be too proud to learn from the florist, or to plant what is so obviously beautiful people forget to recommend it; in this case, the flower which defined a certain range of blue.

I intend soon (taking a tip from the florist's bucket) to try out #3, the safflower, *Carthamus tinctorius*,

* Numbers in the text refer to the seed list on page 82.

whose other name, the saffron thistle, reminds us what it is – that orange thistle which sometimes, on reaching London, seems to have had too crushing a ride.

It is the full orange I want, no lame excuse for a hue. People are sometimes under the illusion that the flowers they find ugly, or over-assertive, are the ones that have been genetically modified. In point of fact, the flowers they find ugly are very often orange, like the incomparable #4, Californian poppy, *Eschscholzia californica*. When I first invited visitors to my garden, they turned the corner and very loudly and flatly declared, 'I don't like *that*.' Perhaps I had let it seed itself too promiscuously, but I have charted its favour in the last decade. Today I think people would say more tactfully: 'Orange can sometimes be so difficult to *place*.'

It means the same thing. It means I don't like orange: it 'fires a gun'. But I remember one summer, in the august Venetian courtyard of the Isabella Stewart Gardner Museum in Boston, all the window-boxes had been filled with trailing #5, nasturtiums, *Tropaeolum majus*, the seed we are given to plant as children because it is large enough to handle individually: it is childproof. Presented so assertively and in such numbers, the nasturtiums dismissed any doubts about their worthiness.

For this list I choose the admirable 'Alaska' with its variegated leaves, and no two leaves ever the same, each one a masterpiece. In my garden we try to accommodate any variety of nasturtium we can find. Some we grow from seed, some from tubers. Nor do I like a year to pass without the orange ice-lolly flowers of the tall **#6**, Mexican sunflower, *Tithonia rotundifolia*. 'Torch' is the full-size variety. I first became aware of it on a visit to Monet's garden at Giverny, but I have no idea whether Monet would actually have grown it. The striking thing about Monet's garden – the part of it which fronts the house, not the water-garden – is its brightness, its obviousness.

And you see how obvious my taste is. I like a flower the colour of blue poster-paint, **#7** *Phacelia campanularia*, the Californian bluebell, of the purest lemon-yellow like **#8**, *Oenothera biennis*, the evening primrose. I like the plants of childhood, like **#9**, love-in-a-mist, *Nigella damascena*, and **#10**, forget-me-not, *Myosotis sylvatica*. This leaves us so far notably short on reds and pinks, but not chronically short with ninety more to go.

flowers
for
their
size

ENGLAND

'I love flowers,' says a friend, 'but I don't like *plants*.'
I can easily understand the distinction. Plants involve
mess and responsibility and edaphic ('of or pertaining
to the soil') requirements. They perhaps expect a
commitment of us that we are not, at this stage in our
lives, prepared to give. Flowers can seem to come out
of nowhere. Bought, arranged, admired, chucked out –
they are given no chance to reproach us. Arum lilies
are like this: spotless, exotic, unreal. One can tell
from his photographs that Robert Mapplethorpe loved
flowers. One hardly expects him to have liked plants.

Among the plants for people who don't really like
plants is the recently popular category called
'architectural'. What is an architectural plant? It is
something big, and possibly expensive, and of a bold
shape – above all something that promises to make an
immediate and permanent impact on the space we are
filling – but its resemblance to actual architecture
may be minimal. A stand of bamboo does not remind
me of any architecture I know, even though I have
lived in countries where much of the architecture
uses bamboo. And what building looks like a
phormium?

If I gaze up at a giant hogweed (*Heracleum
mantegazzianum*, a plant which we may not grow –

an irresponsible plant), I may indeed be reminded of gothic fan vaulting. But a giant hogweed is not an architectural plant in the popular sense, because by the end of the year it is going to let us down: this beautiful structure will die back. I might add that if the giant hogweed looks architectural in its structure, then so do many umbellifers of different scale: cow-parsley, dill, and (a crop failure for us last year) *Ammi majus*, which is referred to in one of my books as false bishop's weed. (False bishops! When have you ever met a bishop who wasn't false?)

Still, if we are to be thwarted in our ambitions to have the giant hogweed romping around the periphery, the angelicas are there as our reward, the grand old sentinels of vegetable gardens. I would choose #11, the oriental *Angelica gigas*, purple-stemmed and purple-flowered, although we have found it to be monocarpic (that is, it dies after flowering).

In general, experimenting with various angelicas, we have found them easiest to keep going by shaking the seeds out of the ripe seedheads and allowing them to grow where they fall (they do not remain viable long). A plant, then, which may take a couple of years to reach full size. There follows one summer of glory, before it goes over. Such a habit cannot easily be accommodated in the kind of garden in which every scrap of space is supposed to be maximally active, year in, year out.

All those umbels, all those umbellules ... My
garden is the subject of crazes, but with an underlying
tendency towards the encyclopedic. So the umbellifer
craze makes an investment of time and space in #12,
the giant fennel, *Ferula communis*, obligatory, given
the prospect of an eventual (they say) five-metre
flower-spike (only likely under Mediterranean
conditions). I am warned that it may be advisable to
remove this spike before large amounts of seed are set,
to keep the plant perennial. But what we want from
such plants is the spectacle they offer as they go, so
we must pay for this.

With anything that grows really, really fast and
large in a temperate climate, there is likely to be a
price to pay. A ceanothus will romp up a wall, but its
wood and its roots will be vulnerable to wind. The
wonderfully obliging #13, *Abutilon vitifolium*, which
is a ten-foot-tall woody mallow, coming with white or
lavender flowers, similarly produces a wood which
needs the protection of a wall. After a few years,
although the stem is thick at the base, the whole
becomes overdeveloped and ungainly. If something
puts on six foot of growth in a year, one cannot expect
that growth to be of the quality of, say, teak. The
abutilon makes a bargain with us: it grows fast, and
can easily be replaced from its own seed. But it does
need replacing – it is not 'architectural'.

When I look at #14, the shoo-fly plant, *Nicandra
physaloides*, growing self-sown in the surface of my

drive, with its feet in 'as-dug' ballast over concrete rubble over clay, I think to myself: somewhere in the world this thing must be an utter menace. Peru is its home – it is the apple of Peru, with its blue and white flowers and its black seed-cases – seeds that can lie dormant for decades, they do say. I am happy that these come back, and happy (although I do not bank on it) to see the tobacco plants return, especially #15, *Nicotiana sylvestris*.

I used to believe, in principle, that the only sunflower worth growing would be the traditional, and the tallest type. But I was converted by Sarah Raven's catalogue, a short but growing and well-thought-out selection of seeds aimed for the flower arranger, to #16, *Helianthus annuus* 'Valentine', with lemon-yellow petals and a dark centre. What you lose in height (not much, admittedly) you gain in flower power. You must stake these things, or they fall over and uproot themselves.

#17, *Salvia sclarea*, is important for us in early summer, and seeds itself around, offering tall pale bracts. You want hazy? It does hazy, sure. Hazy and tall is the Scotch thistle, #18, *Onopordum acanthium*, brother to #19, the milk thistle, *Silybum marianum*. And may I mention another plant that 'fires a gun': #20, *Lychnis chalcedonica*, Maltese cross, for scarlet in the palette, which I failed to squeeze into the previous chapter?

[#15]

flowers
that
hop
around

All but the tidiest, most obsessively controlling of gardeners look forward to those plants that hop around. At first they are placed near the front of the border. Next they find their way out on to the path, into the gravel or the cracks in the paving. And the first time this happens one thinks: now my garden is beginning to show that extra panache – this is maturity in miniature, and these will be my signature plants.

They could be something special, they could be nothing out of the ordinary. At first I used to wonder what was the name of the tiny bronze clover-leaved oxalis, which you often see in front gardens. A 'cosmopolitan weed', the dictionary calls it, *Oxalis corniculata*, the procumbent yellow sorrel. Soon I discovered I had acquired it anyway, along with another classic, the fern-leaved yellow fumitory, *Corydalis lutea*, which is so flattering to a new retaining wall. A third of these, the ivy-leaved toadflax, with its purple and yellow snapdragon flowers, soon followed unbidden.

Less commonly seen is #21, *Omphalodes linifolia* or Venus's navelwort. Grey-leaved and with spikes of white flowers, this twelve-inch annual brings with it thoughts of broderie anglaise, white needlework on

white, the underwear of the
high-minded. The first
sowing might be in
spring, but at the end of its
season the drying spikes are cut
down and laid in my garden
wherever we think we could do with
some more of this charmer. The seeds
ripen and fall out, and by autumn the new
seedlings are showing. Gertrude Jekyll
reckoned this for cutting.

   Now if this grey and white scheme
we'd be fired up with black, the
Viola 'Bowles's Black', is the truly valuable
self-seeder. Inevitably black with green in
isolation, it enjoys tooling around with more
violas, keen on bloodlines, one wow! Here we
should argue out the less perfectly black
seedlings but in most the charming fact, I
find of the music of white happens somewhere
else with the stir of profusely seeding itself is
the purple-green leaved *Labiatowitz*, the
Labrador violet.

   This sorrow-black velvet-green fine garden
can't go on for too life. And lost, like the massacre
suppose, in a cloud of purple-blue, should be a self-sown
always-back crab of delphiniums minded like Pygmy
This noisy in its blown purple-like is of a different

...wers. It seeded itself and has been
coming back, in a raised bed, in a bed
and between paving, ever since. A
perennial that can behave like
an annual: it survives winters
in places like Siberia and
Mongolia. There are other
strains of *D. grandiflorum*
should this one prove elusive.
Another potter for the small bouquet,
this is a naturally short delphinium, not some
perverse plant-breeder's mean-minded fantasy.

For a very small Californian poppy, #24,
Eschscholzia caespitosa 'Sundew', about the smallest
poppy I have grown, and I have lost it through
allowing it to be crowded out. But I shall try it again,
sown in a raised bed in a warm spot, and next time
without competition. The 'Sundew' in its name
denotes a particularly pale yellow strain, but I should
be equally happy with the species.

For its foliage, and particularly for the way its
variegated rosettes of thistle leaves keep growing
through the winter months (the huge cardoon offers
the same out-of-season interest), #25, *Galactites
tomentosa* recommends itself. Don't think of moving
this biennial plant (should such be available). It doesn't
like that. And don't. They say, be disappointed on
seeing the plant in flower, because that (unusually)
happens to be its worst time of the year. But

you must let it flower, because you must let it seed itself around. The suggestion of milk in the name refers to the incomparable white veining of the leaves, which are tomentose (woolly) underneath.

Thrift next, that is, **#26**, *Armeria maritima*, the sea-pink which, on cliff-tops, is normally grazed or windswept to a close turf, but which in the garden grows into luxuriant hummocks. Ignore the opinion of the Revd William Hanbury that the 'withered heads and stalks will much injure the beauty of those in bloom, and have a dull, indolent and disagreeable look'. You want those withered heads to seed themselves in the cracks, so that you can then chuck out the old cushions. 'It is a foolish man dead-heads his thrift.' (Spurious old proverb.)

Foolish too is the impulse to tidy up **#27**, *Pulsatilla vulgaris*, the Pasque flower, for the seed-heads are beautiful (like those of the clematis), and the ripe seed is best sown fresh, or allowed to spread itself around. Still, given a large enough supply, one would like to cut this rare (but not difficult) wild flower for the house.

#28, chives, *Allium schoenoprasum*: obvious, yes, but it is better to be obvious (and have a supply of chives) than to be subtle (and purchase triangular packs at irritating prices). And besides, it is traditional to have chives growing by the kitchen door.

A prolific corydalis, less frequently found than the yellow fumitory mentioned above, is **#29**,

flowers that hop around

C. cheilanthifolia. The specific name means that it has leaves like the lip fern, cheilanthes. Tinged bronze in spring, with yellow flowers, it participates in that clothing of the as-yet unclad spaces, and is as welcome therefore as #30, *Erigeron mucronatus*, a Mexican daisy and the quintessential plant for hopping around.

I admit that, with hummocks of thrift and clumps of chives and all the rest of these flowers growing in the paving around the back door, you need an almost Ethiopian agility when running in from the garden to answer the telephone. Cordless phones are the answer, not tidy paving.

flowers for cutting

. Taste has changed greatly over the last ten years, and the list of flowers we feel like growing reflects that change. Some of the change has been consciously campaigned for in the gardening press: there has been an entertaining running battle mounted by Christopher Lloyd against received wisdom and ghastly good taste, against the timid palette of so many gardens. At the same time, and perhaps less noticed, there is the effect of fashion in interior decorating.

If you look at what is proposed, in clever, design-conscious shops, as a flower vase today (indeed if you look at the common colours of many modern household objects), it is not surprising that the flowers we would choose to fill these vases come from a different list from the ones we would have chosen for the home a few years ago. And it is inevitable that, if a certain flower begins to look good in the house, it will in time begin to look good again in the garden.

The alternative hypothesis would be that we will have a range of city flowers, for deployment in interiors, and country flowers, for the great outdoors. This supposes that the modern designer's passion for brightly coloured daisies such as gerberas will be confined to the city section of the brain, while old roses will continue to thrive in the country section. However, this is not happening. The same newspapers and magazines are read in city and country.

I well remember a gardening friend, ten years ago, saying gently and forgivingly, 'Now, what's all *that* about?' gazing into a bed in which common marigolds had been allowed to get, perhaps, out of hand. But the common pot marigold can hold its own extremely well in a common modern vase. *Calendula officinalis* is the name, and I recommend as **#31** the strain called 'Indian Prince'.

For a vivid illustration of this shift in floral taste, you can compare two books which would seem to be addressing the same subject. *The Flower Arranger's Garden* by Rosemary Verey (Conran Octopus, 1989) presents us with plans for borders and island beds which, without undue disturbance, can be plundered for the house. But you would have to be very clever to guess, just from looking at them, that these designs had been made with the flower arranger in mind. The emphasis is on shrubs and perennials, and only a handful of annuals makes its way into the list of essential flowers.

By comparison, *The Cutting Garden* by Sarah Raven (Frances Lincoln, 1996) proposes a kind of design in which the function of the plot announces itself boldly. Flowers are planted in straight lines, as they might be in allotments, or in frank, comprehensible clumps. This is more than what the Americans sometimes call a posy patch: it could well constitute your whole garden. But if every flower is chosen with an eye to its usefulness for cutting, it follows – or it seems to follow – that the list of flowers will be different from those you would expect in a garden laid out without such a purpose in mind.

Many flowers mentioned earlier in this series come into such a scheme: basic, apparently simple-minded choices like cornflowers, nasturtiums, love-in-a-mist, forget-me-nots, sunflowers and delphiniums. And perhaps to some tastes the list, when set out like that, might begin to look infantile. Who can imagine that it is sophisticated to grow snapdragons? Perhaps it is not. But when I first saw the buckets full of giant snapdragons for sale in New York, I wondered why I was not growing #32, *Antirrhinum majus*, in my garden. You need an F1 Hybrid seed for the full three-foot scale.

Flowers that remind one of hot continental summers include the Mexican sunflower mentioned previously at #6, *Tithonia rotundifolia*, which always brings back Giverny for me, and #33, *Cosmos bipinnatus* 'Purity', the white version. We grow the crimson 'Dazzler' as well. These we tend to dot around the borders, where they do especially happily in warm summers, as does the spider flower, #34, *Cleome spinosa*, available in purple, pink and white.

South America and the West Indies are where it is at home. It packs a mean thorn.

These are plants which have earned their place in the garden, long before the question of cutting them arose. And the same is true of that native of Texas and Louisiana, **#35**, *Gaura lindheimeri*: you want to see it waving in the breeze, giving a pink shimmer to the border, long before you want – if indeed you do – to see it in a vase. But I would think twice before letting **#36**, the zinnias, out of the posy patch. These are what you see grown in straight rows in France, and that is how they look good – or in a simple jug. Cactus-flowered are the ones we grow.

Always on the lookout for things to grow near roses, and hoping that they will be long-flowering, I was delighted last year with **#37**, *Salvia viridis* 'Blue', from Sarah Raven's list. The blue is in the bracts, brilliant Moroccan blue the catalogue calls it, and puts it in the top ten for foliage. It will seed itself around, which is one reason why I want it. Another reason is its flowering season – May

flowers for cutting

to October. This used to be called *S. horminum*. That it lasts indefinitely in a vase is a prospect that gives me the horrors.

Sweet scabious, **#38**, or *Scabiosa atropurpurea*, which some do call Egyptian rose, though truth to tell it is South African: one for the Black Garden, it grew generously for us. Among the numerous columbines, Chiltern Seeds is offering **#39**, *Aquilegia alpina* 'Hensol Harebell', a particularly desirable blue. And, if obliged to restrict myself to one sweet pea, **#40** would be the one listed by Sarah Raven as *Lathyrus* 'Matucana' (syn. 'Cupani's Original'), and 'Cupani' in the addendum to the Chiltern Seeds catalogue. This pea was sent in 1699 from Sicily to the grammar school in Enfield, an auspicious start to a distinguished and influential career.

the
perennial
prejudice

If you look at the lists of gardening books in print, you will find that the volumes devoted to perennials notably outnumber those concerned with annuals and biennials. And if you look at the volumes devoted to annuals, you may well find that they are not really devoted to annuals at all, but to bedding plants which may or may not be, strictly speaking, annuals.

And this fact has some significance. For a part of the neglect of annuals in the gardening press may be put down to an ancient dislike of bedding plants, which were associated with badly run parks. According to this prejudice – for that is what it has become – the foundation of good gardening is the abandoning of bedding plants in favour of perennials and shrubs. And according to a recent, more extreme version, the foundation of good gardening is the abandonment of everything (shrubs, annuals, bulbs, the lot) except perennials: the aim is to create vast perennial ecologies, prairies at the bottom of the garden.

Do you believe in prairies? They may prove an awesome undertaking, and perhaps in the end a somewhat boring prospect; a horror, potentially, if not done well. But then, the same applies to any gardening style.

My strong preference is for a garden, as it were, 'open to all the talents' – and that is why I always

pay particular attention to
the minority of garden writers
who look seriously at annuals
and biennials. This has nothing to
do with bedding schemes (which I
am very happy to see done well), but
everything to do with getting to know
and use the full range of possible
plants available.

Some of these flowers are going to die on us
after one (annuals) or two (biennials) years. If this
fact is too dismaying to contemplate, you have an
annuals problem. If the dismay derives simply from
the thought that all your planting will have to be done
over again, you are overlooking a range of
obliging plants which will indeed come
back again, and in profusion. An
obvious example is #41, the
common foxglove, *Digitalis
purpurea*, which will seed
itself and come back, being
biennial, every other year,
and will grow happily
under trees and bushes.
Excessive devotion to
perennials would cut
you off from this
pleasure, as from the
delights of #42,

the perennial prejudice

honesty, *Lunaria annua*. Both the purple honesty and the pink foxglove have their white versions. Do you want to live without these? Do you want to live without honesty?

Another biennial which we allow to colonize a clump of blackthorns is the beautiful umbellifer, #43, *Smyrnium perfoliatum*. When it is performing, the upper part of the plant turns a yellowy green, so that a drift of smyrnium gives the illusion of a pool of sunlight in a wood.

A similar yellow green is offered by another umbellifer, or annual herb for full sunlight, #44, dill or *Anethum graveolens*. It is a colour found useful by hip florists, who also turn to a self-sowing perennial, #45, lady's mantle or *Alchemilla mollis*. Chiltern Seeds offers a version of this called *A. mollis* 'Robustica', which is the one for cut flowers.

And in the context of so much yellow, and such prolific self-sowing, I must mention a perennial member of the poppy family, *Chelidonium majus*, and its double version, #46, *C. majus* 'Flore Pleno'. Chelidonium, known as the greater celandine, is a flower of the hedgerow. My seed I collected outside Holy Trinity Church, Brompton Road, beloved of evangelical city slickers (the church, that is). The flower may be too evangelical for some tastes: it certainly spreads the word.

If one was told of an annual which grew to around six feet, had flowers like pink coal-scuttles and smelt

of 1950s hair oil, would the prospect be attractive? I
like #47, *Impatiens glandulifera*, or, as Chiltern Seeds
has it, *I. roylei* – Himalayan Balsam – well enough. It
reminds me of the banks of the Wear in Durham, with
its exploding seed-capsules. But it is super-prolific,
and I should not mention it without saying that it is
much best introduced into a wild part of the garden, if
such is available.

Turn to that essential work of garden reference,
Annuals and Biennials by Roger Phillips and Martyn
Rix (Macmillan, 1999) and you will find eight pages
with illustrations devoted to *Impatiens*. And these are
by no means all busy Lizzies (versions of *I.walleriana*)
but include many yellow-flowered species from damp
places in China, and some with no names yet.

Like the other volumes by Phillips and Rix,
Annuals and Biennials shows photographs not only of
the individual plants but also in many cases of the
way these grow in their spectacular natural habitats,
such as the Mojave desert, Cape Province, or the
Himalayan foothills. One gets an idea – whether
rightly or not – of the way these flowers might be
persuaded to grow naturally in the garden.

Any flower can be made to look ridiculous, through
ridiculous planting. One remembers the solemn way
in which borders were edged with alternating plants of
alyssum and lobelia. Yet #48, sweet alyssum,
Lobularia maritima, grows happily enough when
taken out of this context and allowed to seed itself

quietly in
some crack or other,
at the foot of a wall, or in
some paving. And I like
finding **#49**, *Lobelia erinus*,
growing where some pot or other
once stood.

This is one way in which annuals
make themselves a perennial feature of the
garden. That is not to say that we should expect
them all to oblige in the same way, to relieve us of
the obligation to think things afresh. It is just that
some flowers, such as the charming
blue woodruff, **#50**, *Asperula
orientalis*, can be relied on to
remember to renew themselves,
even if we forget.

useful
and
decorative
herbs

This book began with the proposition that it might be a good idea to look at the kind of garden that could be made, on any site from a balcony upwards, using only a hundred packets of seed. I have so far avoided flowers which, although they could well in theory be raised from seed, are much better acquired as plants.

The point is not to make things harder. The point, to recap, is to look at the flower garden at the beginning of the season as if it were a vegetable garden and ask simply: what do I want to grow this year? Forget design for a moment. Design has become a terrible, stupid and expensive tyrant. The emphasis here is all on content. Such a flower garden should have the same beauty as an allotment. It says: this is what I felt like having this year.

If I feel like making myself an omelette fines herbes, I need equal quantities of finely chopped parsley, tarragon, chives and chervil. But where do I get the chervil? It is the slenderest, most delicate and wilting of herbs, and I really must grow it if I am to have it. So, for this reason alone, chervil takes its place as #51, *Anthriscus cerefolium*. Cow parsley's kid brother, it will make no great impact on the garden, but the garden is where you need to have it.

Chives have already appeared as #28 on this list (as

has dill, **#44**). For tarragon I would purchase a plant. Parsley, **#52**, *Petroselinum crispum*, is of great interest in the flower garden, and by parsley I mean the curly-leaved traditional variety. On the allotment, when it runs to seed, it may seem a nuisance, but when it seeds itself near the kitchen door it is both handy and handsome. That green is beautiful. That leaf is beautiful in the border too.

Another herb which you have to grow from seed if you are to have it is **#53**, summer savory, *Satureja hortensis*. There is one thing to do with it (apart from various supposed medicinal uses with which I have no patience), but that one thing is excellent: it is served chopped with young broad beans, dressed with olive oil or butter. It is an annual like chervil. Winter savory, *Satureja montana*, its perennial cousin, is a nice thing, but not really a substitute.

Sorrel, **#54**, *Rumex acetosa*, you will sometimes see in the shops, but packaged in such mean quantities one wonders what the vendors can possibly have in mind. This is a leaf that, on the slightest contact with heat, dissolves into a gunge. A handful, stewed in butter, reduces almost to nothing. This 'nothing' fills an omelette, or gets added to a chicken stock for a sorrel soup. For those Jane Grigsonish moments of summer, this is what you need. Again, the only practical way is from seed.

Lovage, *Levisticum officinale*, comes in at **#55**, although you may prefer to buy a small plant. It will stay with you, putting on a good six foot of growth in a year, before dying back. Like many of my favourite garden plants, it is an umbellifer, and it stands happily at the back of the flower border. The leaves are chopped into a salad when young – later in the season they will become too tough and strong-tasting. The flavour is like celery. The books say it goes in casseroles or stocks. Take my advice: it will easily overwhelm a stock. Used in a salad, it stands up very well to a strong dressing of anchovy, garlic, lemon and olive oil. One is told to cut the stems back to provide a fresh supply of young leaves. But I like to have one or two salads in early summer, and then enjoy the plant for its gigantism.

What is borage for? *Borago officinalis*, **#56**, is for distributing small flowers of pure sky blue around the garden. Admittedly, these blue flowers can look pretty in a salad, and there is the whole business of Pimm's. But does anybody really grow borage in order to add a cucumber taste to Pimm's, when a slice of cucumber would do the trick just as well? Borage is a really useful and friendly self-seeder, an incomparable addition to the garden's informal look. The white version may be thought to miss the point somewhat, but it too is welcome with us.

The various forms of culinary sage are normally grown from cuttings, as is rosemary, although the latter has seeded itself in my paving, and grown well there along with different thymes. And this reminds one that a plant such as the common lavender, although easily bought, can be raised in quantity from seed, and that if you wanted a hedge of, for instance, **#57**, *Lavandula spica* (or *angustifolia*) 'Hidcote Blue', this would be one way of acquiring it.

I take it that basil is more of a plant for the house, the window-sill, than for the garden in Britain. Even there, one is lucky to achieve anything approaching the herb as it grows in a hot climate. When I bought a bunch of basil from a farmer's market in New York, I was stopped in the street, it was so spectacular: woody at the base, and pungent enough to leave its smell on your hands and clothes. *Ocimum basilicum*, **#58**, is the name: one can but try and try again. Chiltern Seeds lists almost twenty varieties.

Two final umbellifers for their garden beauty: sweet fennel, *Foeniculum vulgare*, in its bronze form, is **#59**, a plant to smell in the heat of a Mediterranean day; and at **#60**, sweet Cicely, *Myrrhis odorata*, known once as cow chervil, sweet-humlock, sweets or British myrrh – 'very good for old people that are dull and without courage; it rejoiceth and comforteth the heart and increaseth their lust and strength'.

A likely story.

the
micro-
meadow

FernSeed

COMMUNIS (5880)

ERUM COMMUNIS, Cumbria, LA12

Bortree Sule, Ulverston, Cumbria,

Everyone is attracted by the idea of a meadow, or by the notion that meadow conditions can be imitated in the garden. A few discouraging but realistic remarks might be helpful. One thing I never see emphasized is that a meadow – a real meadow, that is – is a field with a product. If you have no use for the product, the hay, you are likely to have a problem with a meadow.

I recently read an admirable account of a garden grown largely for the benefit of insects: every plant was rated according to the number and variety of insects it attracted. Towards the end, the author admitted that, finding it hard to compost the hay from her garden, she had the local council cart it away instead. But there must be something wrong with the ecology of growing hay for council infill sites.

Another thing that sets my teeth on edge when meadow-enthusiasts describe what they have done is the insistence that, since meadow flowers grow best on poor soil, you should lower the fertility of your soil before you begin. So far, so justifiable. But they go on to say that, if necessary, you should remove the fertile topsoil before sowing your meadow seed mixture.

I protest. Who is handing out this destructive advice, and who is listening to it? Who is carting away his or her fertile topsoil, and what are they finding underneath, when they have done so? What plants, what bulbs, what seeds are being carted away? And what have they done wrong?

It is only from the specialist point of view of the gardener that a meadow must have low fertility. An actual working meadow, which is supposed to grow a crop of grass for cattle, may have at least two obvious sources of fertility. It may have clover. Does the meadow-gardener propose to exclude clover from the mix, on the grounds that it introduces too much nitrogen into the soil?

The second source of fertility is of course animals. 'Sheep eat the grass, then dung the ground for more,' wrote that admirable poet George Herbert, describing a desirable aspect of providence. A meadow is grown for its hay. When that is cut, and the grasses have grown again, the field is grazed. Among the beneficial effects (from the point of view of the meadow gardener) of this grazing is the fact that the cattle tread the new seed into the ground. Indeed, one way in which you can turn a cultivated field into a meadow, and which we have practised on my farm with some success, is to take the hay from another meadow and spread it over the target area, and then put cattle on it. The cattle both eat the hay (or not, if they don't feel like it) and tread it under foot.

The easiest way to start a meadow is to take a field or patch of lawn and put it under a meadow regime:

the micro-meadow

no fertilizers, pesticides or herbicides, no animals to graze it, no mower to touch it before the first cut of the year – and this cut to come only after the seeds of the desirable wildflowers have been allowed to ripen. Meadows, like lawns, arise through management, and this is the basic management for a wildflower meadow. The results are to be appreciated over years, decades even.

In fields where fertilizers were once used, the effect will wear off reasonably quickly. Obviously, if the farmer was applying fertilizer annually, he was doing so because an annual application was necessary for the effects he wished to achieve (fertilizers are expensive). So the effect is reversible, to some extent at least. To make a wildflower meadow on such a site, it is better to try the new management system, and see where it leads.

An old neglected field which I bought to add to the farm, and which I knew to contain many cowslips and perhaps some other interesting flowers, was (on professional advice) gone over once with a disc harrow, so that the surface of the soil was disturbed but the turf was not entirely destroyed. Then it was rolled assiduously, to produce a ground so firm that, we were instructed, a bicycle should not leave a track in it. On to this firm surface we sowed our grass and wildflower mix. In the first year, the field was cut early, in order to stop unwanted annuals, such as thistles, from seeding. So it wasn't until the second year that we could really tell how successful our efforts had been.

It turned out that we were very successful indeed. The field retains its cowslips, which have spread fast, and some eccentricities from its former life – such as patches of daffodils. I should not be surprised one year to find orchids there, because they would certainly have been there in the past. And the way we are managing the field is designed to encourage them if they are there, as they are on other parts of the farm. Note that in all this we have made no attempt to eliminate the coarser grasses, either by ploughing or by weedkilling or by (supposing this to have been feasible on a large scale) the removal of topsoil. The four meadows we have, each one somewhat different in character and history, have been developed on the basis of what we found there in the first place.

This kind of perennial meadow is distinct from the vision you tend to see in blurry pastel photographs, in which poppies, cornflowers and corncockle give an 'impressionist' effect. The annual flowers blooming in such fields are the weeds of cornfields, and in order to bloom readily they need a cornfield regime. But this implies annual ploughing – and this is very far from the repertory of most gardeners.

However, what is possible – and much easier to achieve than a really satisfactory perennial wildflower meadow (which should be viewed as a long-term project) – is a micro-meadow of annual flowers, grown

the micro-meadow

in a small patch. Two years ago we did this, and the reaction of visitors was always at first to laugh at the small scale of our project: intended as a cornfield with traditional extras, it measured only six paces by two.

The corn we took from a handful or two of mixed birdseed – a mistake, since such seed may often be heat-treated, which destroys its viability. The wildflowers came from a couple of packets of wildflower mix, available in any garden centre, together with the things we particularly wanted: cornflowers (which have featured early in this list as #2), #61, *Agrostemma githago* or corncockle, and #62, *Papaver rhoeas* or field poppy.

The ground was prepared in April and the seed mixture scattered over. In the early stages, some obvious weeds were removed, while others, like the purple-flowered wall fumitory, *Fumaria muralis*, were left. A dominant presence among the flowers, along with the cornflowers and poppies, was corn chamomile, *Anthemis arvensis*. In due course we had a spectacular display, but little evidence of corn in our field.

Later I was reading the introduction to *Annuals and Biennials*, the important book by Roger Phillips and Martyn Rix which I have already mentioned, when I came across this sentence: 'Poppies, cornflowers, corn-cockle and *Nigella*, combined with some grasses, umbelliferae and white daisies, will make a fine scheme to recreate a neolithic Mediterranean cornfield.' This was indeed what we had achieved, with just the sort of poor germination of corn that neolithic man might have expected in a bad year, but with compensating blooms of **#63**, *Leucanthemum vulgare* or ox-eye daisy.

Chiltern Seeds offers **#64**, a Mixture of Annual Varieties, and **#65**, a Mixture of Perennial Varieties, which could serve as a basis for two such miniature schemes. Of interest as well is **#66**, their California Wildflower mixture. Phillips and Rix go on to say that 'Californian annuals include the wonderful blue and purple *Phacelia* and the pale blue *Nemophila*, as well as the different colours of Californian poppies. Lupins, clarkias and white *Oenothera* complete a grouping which could occur in California.'

An article in the March 2001 issue of *The Garden*, the Journal of the Royal Horticultural Society, reports on experiments with this kind of direct sowing. It recommends a thin layer of sand spread over the bed as a weed-suppressing mulch (the seeds being sown on to this sand), and it shows the difference between results with or without a modest use of slug pellets. The authors, Nigel Dunnett and James Hitchmough, calculate that to plant a square metre with herbaceous perennial plants may cost £20–25 at garden centre prices; using seed, the same area comes out at 20–50p.

They tell us that topsoil in a typical garden will contain a 'seed bank' of 10,000 seeds per square metre. These are waiting to germinate when the soil is disturbed. However, a layer of sand of between 5 and 10 millimetres – up to three-eighths of an inch – will reduce weed germination to manageable levels. A single application of slug pellets around the time of the germination of the seeds proved effective, and it was shown that these pellets did not have to be applied all over the sown plot, but only around the edges. Without slug pellets at all, the seedlings suffered 35 per cent damage.

the
poppy
festival

What really gets a regular garden going is not so much a plan as a craze, or a series of overlapping crazes. And when we are in the grips of the craze we want to know everything there is to be known about a plant – how it appears in every variant, what can be done with it, what will make it happy. When the craze subsides, it may be that we can begin to think the unthinkable: to admit, for instance, that we are going to have to live without azaleas, or cut down on our hydrangea habit.

Something will normally survive these crazes, and whatever it is that survives them – whether it is a single species or a group of plants – should take its place among our permanent affections. Maybe a flower does not agitate us any more in the way it used to, but that does not mean we have forgotten it, or become indifferent.

When I first began to put my garden together, it seemed to me that, within the garden, there should be a rose garden, and that somewhere around there should be as many types of iris as could be accommodated. And furthermore, so it seemed to me, there should be lilies in abundance. Obviously roses, irises and lilies were the essential constituents of a flower garden.

So it seemed to me, and so it still seems! But it is years since I added a rose to the mixture, or even looked seriously at the rose catalogues. Irises and lilies are a different matter, for we keep adding to their number, and varying the approach to growing them: sometimes they have been scattered to all corners of the garden, sometimes grouped together, particularly if they are being grown to be cut.

Propagation by seed is not the first consideration in either case, although, given a little patience and space, and given the desire for a large number of lilies, some species are worth growing in this way. That great star of the genus, **#67**, *Lilium regale*, sows itself around in my garden to a modest degree, but in a manner that seems to suggest that one would be foolish to throw away the ripe seed-heads. The Chiltern catalogue says it may flower in the second year from seed. But not nearly at full strength, in our experience. In three years, however, there it is.

A more prolific self-seeder, on a raised bed where we grow it (for it is a small thing, best grown among small plants such as alpines), is *L. formosanum* var. *pricei*. This is a short-stemmed version of plain *L. formosanum*, which others recommend as a biennial, although we have yet to do well with it. Among

several lily seeds, Chiltern offers **#68**,
L. formosanum 'Little Snow White', which
must be the one we grow.

Still, in a garden envisaged as growing from a
hundred packets of seed, neither lilies nor irises will
be the star performing genera. The poppies have far
more to offer – fragile though they may sometimes
seem. That fragility is an illusion. The Spanish poppy,
#69, *Papaver rupifragum*, in what I call pale orange,
may seem of feeble constitution, but it just hangs
around the back door, returning year after year,
looking after itself. We grow **#70**, *P. sendtneri*, in
paving: it is pure white and miniature, and it
does not insist on its native limestone (or
that altitude of 9,000 feet which is
sometimes inconvenient to arrange).

The field poppy (*P. rhoeas*)
mentioned, **#62**, in the previous
chapter earns an honoured place in
the garden in the strain called the
Shirley poppy, which, to be
what the Revd William Wilks
had in mind when he
selected it, ought to be a
single flower in
white, pink or
salmon. Modern
versions delight
in their doubleness.

This kind of annual makes itself a perennial feature of the garden by reliably re-sowing its own patch, as does the tall, incomparable opium poppy, #71, *P. somniferum*, which comes in so many forms, single and double. 'Black Peony' is one I would choose – almost at random. Nothing hangs on your decision, in choosing between the opium poppies. The foliage will all be the same handsome glaucous blue-green. The range of colours – from white through red, pink and purple – seems entirely appropriate to the plant. One is not more virtuous, or more likely to go to heaven, for preferring singles to doubles, or plain to cut-edged petals.

More and more often seen on sale is #72, the Iceland poppy, usually listed as *P. nudicaule*. Its popularity represents a further triumph for the colour orange, for orange is what it does best – a deeper, warmer orange than the Californian poppy, which I listed as #4. The white version, and the intermediate pastel shade, and the yellow, are pleasant variants on the essential orange, the thing itself. This is a flower which astonishes us by being good for cutting, when you would think that it would wilt straight away. (Dipping the cut ends in boiling water is the trick.)

One associates poppies with full sunlight and the heat of early summer, but their range includes the cool and shady. #73, *Meconopsis cambrica*, the yellow Welsh poppy, and its orange and scarlet variants, are self-seeders for shade, flowers that, like the

chelidonium (which is also a kind of poppy), are
expected to get on with it, furnishing shady walks and
gravel paths. I would rave about the blue Himalayan
meconopsis, if I honestly – or plausibly – could claim
to have grown it. Instead, on the blue theme, let me
mention *Corydalis linstowiana* – for corydalis is often
listed as a member of the Papaveraceae – an annual or
biennial which has seeded itself under our roses, with
pale blue flowers. You would have to buy a plant to
start it off.

Two prickly Mexican poppies, #74, *Argemone
mexicana*, and #75, *A. pleiacantha*, the first with
yellow, the second with white flowers (*A. grandiflora*
'White Lustre' is its name in Chiltern's list), suggest
themselves as candidates for a hot Mediterranean-
style garden. Yet we grow the white one among our
roses, which is where I first saw it at Mottisfont. No
doubt in Mexican rose gardens they curse it as a weed.

climbers
on
impulse

At the start of this book, I mentioned a garden I had seen last summer in Manhattan, which consisted of nothing more than morning glories growing up a fire escape. I saw the remains of it again the other day, high above 43rd Street, the dead vines washed grey against the dark metalwork. If I had appreciated it and remembered its location, no doubt I was one of many who had enjoyed it and thought: that was a success.

Suppose it were a success not to be repeated. Suppose the instigator of this garden had simply thought: this year, I feel like seeing morning glories every morning, and for a summer had revelled in the triumph of the project – but the following year were to turn to something else. Would there be something wrong with that?

I imagine the flower forever having a particular association for the owner of this 'garden' – this nondescript container dumped on a fire escape, which suddenly, and so satisfactorily, took off. Whatever the summer of 2000 meant would be summed up by the sight of #76, *Ipomoea tricolor* 'Heavenly Blue'.

To me it means sleeping under a trellis in Greece, but ipomoea is historically associated with Central America. A quick check in the Codex Barberini, an

Aztec herbal now in the Vatican,* gives us the fever flower, *Tontonquixochitl*, and a recipe against hair loss: 'falling hair is checked by washing the head, and if the herb called *xiuhhamolli* is applied to it, ground and cooked in the urine of a dog or a stag, with tree frogs and the small animals *auatecolotl*' (apparently a kind of caterpillar).

What the Codex fails to impart is the recipe for deriving LSD from *Ipomoea tricolor*, which was the standard Aztec hallucinogen. An illustration of the associative power of the flower is the fact that morning glory always lifts the heart, whereas the common white convolvulus (so very familiar in form) always causes it to sink. I have not tried the white version of morning glory ('Pearly Gates') for that reason. There are reds on offer as well. *I. batatas*, as the name more than hints, is the sweet potato.

The smaller the garden, the greater the interest in extending it by means of climbers. Some small town houses have no garden at all, but the house itself has been interpreted as, first and foremost, a support for a rampant clematis or wisteria. I like these examples of horticultural excess very much, but where there is the opportunity to grow just a few more plants it is the smaller climbers that will attract the attention of the

* Martin de la Cruz, *The Badianus Manuscript: An Aztec Herbal of 1552*, introduction, translation and annotations by Emily Walcott Emmart, Johns Hopkins Press, Baltimore, 1940.

climbers on impulse

householder. They are less likely to crowd their neighbours out.

Early on, I mentioned the common nasturtium, *Tropaeolum majus*, grown in the courtyard of a Boston museum, massed in window-boxes. The windows in question are extraordinary, having been transported from Venetian palazzi. The planting might have looked foolish had it been done with anything less than total conviction. As it was, with cascades of nasturtiums, one felt one was seeing the flower used properly for the first time.

An illusion, of course, that the self-confident can create. There are many other tropaeolums, including one that features in that useful book, *Lost Crops of the Incas*,[*] *T. tuberosum*, known to us in the form 'Ken Aslet' (boil the tubers with meat), and to South Americans as *mashua*, a crop for high altitudes which (mark this now) repels many insects and pathogens, and is handy for farmers who can't afford pesticides.

But the tropaeolum I am recommending from seed is #77, the delicate yellow-flowered *T. peregrinum*, canary creeper, which comes from Peru and Ecuador and is for us a half-hardy annual. Another with which we have had success in southern England is #78, *T. ciliatum*, a Chilean, which we have growing up a yew

[*] National Research Council, *Lost Crops of the Incas: little-known plants of the Andes with promise for worldwide cultivation*, National Academy Press, Washington DC, 1989.

hedge, where in Scotland one would more likely see the wonderful flame nasturtium, *T. speciosum*.

Another Chilean/Peruvian, to pursue the theme, is **#79**, *Eccremocarpus scaber*, the glory flower, which is a perfect climber for the small garden since it can climb through a shrub without giving it too much hassle. Orange and red tubular flowers, bright and small, are its contribution. We also grow 'Tresco Cream', which is presumably one of the constituents of Chiltern Seeds' offering, 'Tresco' Mixed. Listed as half-hardy, it is very likely to survive a town winter.

Returning to Mexico we encounter **#80**, the astonishing *Rhodochiton atrosanguineum*, another tender vine, with blood-black flowers (as its specific name warns us to expect) and a surprisingly pronounced calyx. Its colour is similar to that of the popular chocolate cosmos.

Two versions of flowers better known in non-climbing forms. **#81**, *Dicentra scandens*, is a climbing version of Dutchman's breeches, a.k.a. bleeding heart, but with yellow or white heart-shaped flowers. This is a Himalayan perennial. And **#82**, *Aconitum hemsleyanum*, is a Chinese climbing monkshood, and therefore presumably (I haven't tried it) poisonous. The flowers are dark blue, as you'd expect.

Sweet peas I have mentioned earlier in the context of their great ancestor, *Lathyrus cupanii*. **#83** is a blue-flowered pea, *L. sativus* var. *azureus*, known, the books tell me, as Riga or dogtooth pea. And since a mere two peas might sound stingy, I would add a packet of **#84**, Chiltern's Old-fashioned Sweet Peas, Mixed . . . The word old-fashioned in this context holds out an expectation of a better scent than that of more recent varieties, but scent is not my strong point.

Finally **#85**, *Phaseolus coccineus*, is the scarlet runner bean, a plant I am always happy to grow if not obliged so much as to think about eating it. As a flower it is unanswerable, and that is all we need or wish to know about it.

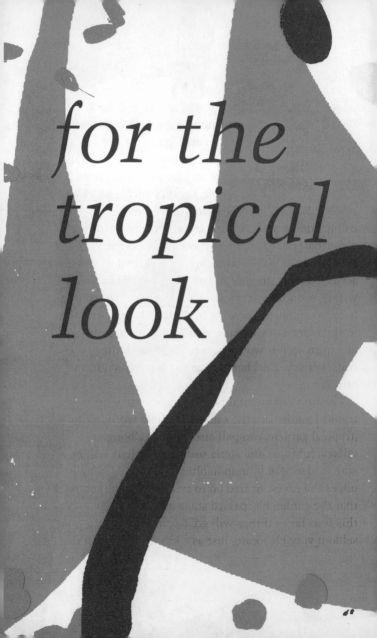

*for the
tropical
look*

The popular and interesting tropical look that has
returned to our gardens, giving a place for certain
flamboyant plants which might previously have failed
a taste test, is the result of an ingenious mix and
match. It does not resemble a real tropical garden very
closely. Rather, it gives an impression of lush
colourfulness and rampant growth, using whatever
plant material suits the fantasy of the designer.

When an actual habitation is established in your
actual tropics, the first plants to surround the house
will be economic staples such as coconut, banana,
bamboo and papaya. None of these will perform for us
in their tropical varieties, although papaya grows so
fast from seed it would be worth trying in the
conservatory. Real bananas are always grown from
offsets.

The first ornamental plants to grace an actual
tropical garden are the same the whole world round
(tropical gardens can pall after a while): bougainvillaea, hibiscus and some sort of impatiens will be
sure evidence of human habitation. Orchids hanging
under the eaves, or tied on to tree trunks, will show
that the garden has passed stage one. But often
this is as far as things will go. Barrio gardens are
seldom very elaborate, just as cottage gardens, in the

days of cottagers, were much less fancy than legend would suggest.

Two flowers of use in the temperate garden, both of which can be grown from seed, are widespread in the tropics. The first is *Lantana camara*, a small shrub with bright flower-heads in a mixture of red, orange and yellow. A kind of verbena, it has become a roadside weed in the tropics. Thompson & Morgan offers #86, *Lantana* 'Camara Mixed Hybrids', while Chiltern Seeds has a dwarf version.

The second is #87, the familiar *Thunbergia alata*, black-eyed Susan, available from both catalogues, a small climber sold here for hanging baskets. The best easily available photo reference book for tropical flowers is the two-volume *Conservatory and Indoor Plants* by Roger Phillips and Martyn Rix (Pan, 1997), a work which is somewhat mislabelled, since it is full of photographs of plants in their natural habitats. Two pages of thunbergias here are enough to provoke the appetite for a flower, climbing or trailing, which turns out surprisingly to be an acanthus relative.

Fundamental to any genuine tropical look are the banana-like, large-leaved heliconias, cannas and ginger lilies. The normal way would be to buy these as plants, but cannas in particular can be raised from seed: #88, *Canna indica*, Indian Shot, is offered again by both catalogues. Cannas don't have to be grown in borders. In the tropics they grow in water very happily, for instance at the edge of a pond, and this is where they can be placed during summers here. Cannas started from fresh seed collected in a garden last summer look fair to flower for us this year.

Last year a friend of mine planted a packet of #89, *Melianthus major*, seed from Chiltern. Of the twelve seeds, ten germinated. She kept two plants, gave one to us and sold the rest, thereby ending the year both popular and in profit. Melianthus is grown in these 'tropical' schemes for its glaucous foliage. Left out of doors it may well survive the winter but it will not flower: the English year does not offer enough heat for it.

But Phillips and Rix show us what it looks like flowering in California, with tall spikes of chocolate flowers in spring (August–September in its native South Africa). What gardeners in England have turned into a herbaceous perennial is by nature a tall, rangy shrub beloved of sunbirds. We are now experimenting with other members of the family, including *M. comosus* (Chiltern). They germinate easily.

Naranjilla, #90, another of the lost crops of the Incas I mentioned in the last chapter, will grow out of doors if given a good start in the greenhouse. *Solanum quitoense* (Chiltern) is its name, and you want it to grow six feet. But even if it doesn't get that far, it will interest you with its bright purple-veined leaves. Supposing it to have ripened its golfball-sized fruit, you can spread the unstrained pulp on your Guatemalan-style cheesecake!

Another solanum, **#91**, goes under the name of poroporo or large kangaroo apple. This is *S. laciniatum*, a raffish, cut-leaved job with egg-shaped fruit, also edible. The whole solanum family seems to have this ambiguous, not entirely respectable, either edible or poisonous (or both, like the potato) character.

Distinctly poisonous is the castor oil plant, **#92**, *Ricinus communis*, the source (if I am not mistaken) of the poison (ricin) in the famous umbrella murder by the KGB of a Bulgarian journalist in London not long ago. Mrs M. Grieve, in *A Modern Herbal* (Penguin reprint), gives a vivid Victorian account of a scientist inadvertently half killing himself with it. It is a Mediterranean plant which has been in English gardens for perhaps half a millennium, perhaps more, but that doesn't stop it looking tropical. We have had best success with a variety called 'Gibsonii'.

Marvel of Peru, *Mirabilis jalapa*, **#93**, was deemed marvellous for producing different-coloured flowers on the same plant. It gave its other name, four o'clock, to the family of Nyctaginaceae. Unless you can grow bougainvillaea, which is improbable in England, you won't have many other Nyctaginaceae in your collection, so why not this easy subtropical weed?

A tropical-style border also featured in the March 2001 issue of *The Garden* features **#94**, *Rehmannia angulata*, the Chinese foxglove. We grow this among the roses, where it does not look out of place. Along

for the tropical look

the same lines, and perhaps more exciting, #95 is *Isoplexis isabelliana* (Chiltern) or, from Thompson & Morgan, you could try *I. sceptrum*. These last three share a page in Phillips and Rix, vol. 2.

as an after-thought

Looking back on this list, which draws from flowers that have been grown from seed and enjoyed in my garden over the last ten years or so, I can see some surprising gaps. Wot no dianthus? Neither the cottage pinks nor the lusher carnations? Well, we haven't got on to carnations, and our cottage pinks, of which we have many, have all been bought or given us as plants and propagated from cuttings. *Dianthus barbatus*, sweet William, comes in at **#96** as being, par excellence, the dianthus to grow from seed, as a biennial, among the roses.

I would have mentioned, had the seed been simpler to find, two small-flowered, long-stemmed Balkan types, *D. cruentus* and *D. giganteus*: the bloody and the gigantic respectively. The RHS encyclopedia is rude about the only yellow wild species, *D. knappii*, calling it 'unattractive of habit', as if it picked its nose. But I like it, and I see the Chiltern catalogue has it and is enthusiastic. Then there are the ground-hugging alpine types, one of which, *D. deltoides*, the maiden pink, has spread happily by seed. Of this, a deep scarlet variety called 'Flashing Light' or 'Leuchtfunk' surely earns its place, **#97**.

Of the many seeds spread by birds, not all are welcome, but some get left for amusement's sake.

There are one or two bird-sown asparagus plants allowed to grow in the rose garden, on the grounds that, if asparagus fern looks right in a bridegroom's buttonhole, the thing itself can hardly look wrong among rose-bushes. But I wouldn't defend this reasoning to the death.

When a truly distinguished plant adopts your garden, it is flattering. The wild spurge laurel, *Daphne laureola*, brought along by a friend who was ditching nearby, has become a presence for us. One might think it wouldn't like our clay. One would be wrong. It turns up everywhere, a harmonious, low evergreen daphne. The handsome cousin of the cuckoo pint, **#98**, *Arum italicum* var. *pictum*, seems to find a place under every shrub, as a matter of course.

And then there was the question whether the foxtail lily, **#99**, the amazing huge *Eremurus robustus*, would do for us what I had read it did in another rose garden (Hyde Hall, I think): seed itself and produce its eight-foot spikes of flowers among shrub roses. I wondered whether the leaves of the eremurus would get enough light in these conditions to thrive.

The answer is that the leaves, which have been heaving through the soil in enormous, almost worrying buds, all through March, get enough of a start in spring and early summer,

as an afterthought

before the competition shades them over. In nature, they die anyway before the plant flowers. But one must have patience, or have other things to think about during the three or four years the seedlings take to grow to flowering size.

One should indeed have other things to think about – ninety-nine other things to think about once I have added #100, the willow gentian, *Gentiana asclepiadea*, to the list. I choose it as being not too choosy to be happy with me: a tallish thing, two foot or so, rather than the ground-hugging kind, happy in shade and almost any soil.

I think that this was the kind of gentian D. H. Lawrence had in mind when he wrote his poem 'Bavarian Gentians', since he twice refers in the final version of the poem to the tallness of the stems (*G. bavarica*, the Bavarian gentian, is mat-forming and short). He speaks of 'Bavarian gentians, tall and dark, but dark/darkening the daytime torch-like with the smoking blueness of Pluto's gloom . . .' And he cries, 'Give me a flower on a tall stem, and three dark flames . . .' He was dying, and he considered it a privilege to have such flowers in the house.

Well, that's my list, and I have forgotten the euphorbias, but it is now too late to do anything about it. The closer you look, the worse the omissions will be, and this garden I have proposed – this reckless coming together of plants – will have faults enough for those who wish to find them. Where are the hellebores, the bulbs, the winter interest? Where are the shrubs? Where are the grasses? Where are the tree ferns?

Where are the tree ferns indeed? For the amount of the reader's money I have spent so far on this hypothetical garden – the packets of seed, some topsoil, the odd book – one could purchase perhaps one handsome tree fern and a pot to put it in. *And this might well be the best way forward.*

For about ten times the amount of money I have spent, one might install a new off-the-peg 'landscaped' garden in a new home – that at least was an estimate given recently for a plot five by six metres: you're looking at anything from £2,500 up. The article in question continued: 'If you add a water feature and patio then the price would be from £5,000 upwards. *It is features and mature planting that cost money.*' (My italics.)

Well, yes, it is features that cost money. Maturity costs money. And it is striking that some of the smallest gardens in Britain are the most expensive, per square metre, to achieve, and striking the amount of propaganda that comes at us, through television, through the gardening press, encouraging this level of expenditure.

I'm not in a position to lecture anyone about expenditure: my garden employs one gardener full-time and has benefited over the years from a great deal of part-time assistance. I regret none of the expenditure (even the heroic failures), as long as I think that the money was, in principle, well used. But even the most lavish gardener in Great Britain – as it were, the Duchess of Northumberland – would think twice about spending on the large scale at the same rate per square inch that the amateur urban gardener is encouraged to spend on a small back garden.

the rest of the kit

Every garden can benefit from a reference library, but it does not have to be large. I have mentioned several times volumes in the Garden Plant Series, published by Pan and written by Roger Phillips and Martyn Rix. The single volume on *Annuals and Biennials*, the two on *Perennials* and the one on *Bulbs*, taken together, offer a formidable photographic archive. The two volumes on *Conservatory and Indoor Plants* are much more interesting than you might expect (if you don't have a conservatory). We grow many of the plants in these volumes out of doors. We await *Alpines*.

There is one general work, of great interest to anyone who has been intrigued at all by this book, called *Garden Flowers from Seed*, by Christopher Lloyd and Graham Rice, which was published here by Viking in 1991. This is available from www.amazon.co.uk in the American edition (Timberland Press), or second-hand perhaps from the incomparable www.bibliofind.com. Mr Rice has two other volumes on growing annuals, worth looking for.

I mentioned several times Sarah Raven's Cutting Garden, a catalogue available from Perch Hill Farm,

Brightling, Robertsbridge, East Sussex TN32 5HP, or www.thecuttinggarden.com. There is a book by Dr Raven called *The Cutting Garden* (Frances Lincoln), which I find has a good attitude. The two large seed catalogues I have referred to are Thompson & Morgan, Poplar Lane, Ipswich IP8 3BU, or www.thompson-morgan.com, and the one I have cited most often, Chiltern Seeds. Not illustrated, but extremely wide-ranging and I would say the seeds come cheap, from Bortree Stile, Ulverston, Cumbria LA12 7PB, or www.chilternseeds.co.uk.

I restricted myself to this small number of sources in this book, because I was interested to keep my recommendations to a bare minimum, but that does not mean that we do not use other sources for seed, both large firms and small. Indeed, we are always on the lookout for rare and unusual plants. One useful source is a botanical garden which runs a distribution scheme for seed. I am a member of the Friends of Oxford Botanic Garden (Rose Lane, Oxford OX1 4AZ).

As for equipment, there is a shed, and in this shed there is a bench on which most of the potting work is done. We have a small greenhouse, and some cold-frames. The seeds are kept in an old fridge in the shed. We used to buy sacks of potting compost from the garden centres. But since we have space for a pile of sharp sand, we tend now to buy a sack of multi-purpose compost, and mix it with sand and a little bonemeal, for our own potting mixture.

the rest of the lot

It is a long time since we bought plastic pots. When we have visitors and hold a plant sale we ask if people have spares, and we find that our friends seem only too happy to get rid of old pots (just as we, in our turn, are only too happy to get rid of wire coathangers). So we have sackfuls of old plastic pots. The seeds are started off in these, rather than in seed trays, before being pricked out and potted on. The pricking out is done with a sharpened length of bamboo.

Garden labels are an old problem. It is better to mark them in pencil rather than ink, which fades or gets washed off. Best for marking in pencil are the old-fashioned aluminium labels, but the magpies do find these attractive, and chuck them around. We use white plastic labels which will take pencil markings (not all of them do). A good watering-can, with a fine rose, makes an excellent Christmas gift, and one can always drop hints in that direction. And I hope that this book too will make a welcome Christmas gift, and be good to read and think about during the winter months.

when raising plants from seed

1. Do pay attention to the instructions on the packet, particularly the recommended months for sowing. Sowing seeds early or out of season is not always a good idea. Sometimes you get away with it, but not always.
2. Sow most seeds on to compost in four-inch pots which give them a good depth for their roots. If the seeds are large, cover with compost roughly the same depth as the size of the seed. Water with a fine, upturned rose.
3. Prick the seedlings out singly into individual pots when they are easy to handle. This varies with the type of seedling, but they should be showing their first set of true leaves.
4. Keep all pots and seedlings out of direct sunlight. If once they dry out, you will lose them.
5. When removing seedlings from pots, if they are small, like lobelias, take a small chunk of compost with the dibbler. If they are larger, remove the whole clump from the pot and it will fall apart.

6. When handling seedlings, always hold them by the leaves, not by the stem. Always treat them as gently as possible.

7. Water them with a solution of Cheshunt Compound to stop them damping off (being attacked by fungus). Use a fine upturned rose.

8. Keep young plants in frost-free conditions, again, out of direct sunlight.

9. Gradually acclimatize them to cold weather: 'harden them off' before planting them in the garden.

10. Potted-up seedlings and young plants are given a weekly feed of Phostrogen.

11. Always make sure a young plant is thoroughly watered before it is planted in the garden. A little bonemeal scattered in the hole will help, unless it encourages your dog to dig up the plant.

12. Forcefully remind your cat about the difference between seed-trays and litter-trays.

the seed list

1. *Adonis aestivalis*, pheasant's eye (Ranunculaceae)
2. *Centaurea cyanus*, cornflower (Asteraceae)
3. *Carthamus tinctorius*, safflower (Asteraceae)
4. *Eschscholzia californica*, Californian poppy (Papaveraceae)
5. *Tropaeolum majus* 'Alaska', nasturtium (Tropaeolaceae)
6. *Tithonia rotundifolia* 'Torch', Mexican sunflower (Asteraceae)
7. *Phacelia campanularia*, Californian bluebell (Hydrophyllaceae)
8. *Oenothera biennis*, evening primrose (Onagraceae)
9. *Nigella damascena*, love-in-a-mist (Ranunculaceae)
10. *Myosotis sylvatica*, forget-me-not (Boraginaceae)
11. *Angelica gigas* (Apiaceae)
12. *Ferula communis*, giant fennel (Apiaceae)
13. *Abutilon vitifolium* (Malvaceae)
14. *Nicandra physaloides*, shoo-fly plant, apple of Peru (Solanaceae)
15. *Nicotiana sylvestris* (Solanaceae)

16. *Helianthus annuus* 'Valentine', sunflower (Asteraceae)
17. *Salvia sclarea*, clary (Lamiaceae)
18. *Onopordum acanthium*, Scotch thistle (Asteraceae)
19. *Silybum marianum*, milk thistle (Asteraceae)
20. *Lychnis chalcedonica*, Maltese cross (Caryophyllaceae)
21. *Omphalodes linifolia*, Venus's navelwort (Boraginaceae)
22. *Viola* 'Bowles's Black' (Violaceae)
23. *Delphinium grandiflorum* 'Blauer Zwerg' (Ranunculaceae)
24. *Eschscholzia caespitosa* 'Sundew' (Papaveraceae)
25. *Galactites tomentosa* (Asteraceae)
26. *Armeria maritima*, thrift (Plumbaginaceae)
27. *Pulsatilla vulgaris*, Pasque flower (Ranunculaceae)
28. *Allium schoenoprasum*, chives (Alliaceae)
29. *Corydalis cheilanthifolia* (Fumariaceae)
30. *Erigeron mucronatus*, Mexican daisy (Asteraceae)
31. *Calendula officinalis* 'Indian Prince', pot marigold (Asteraceae)
32. *Antirrhinum majus*, snapdragon (Scrophulariaceae)
33. *Cosmos bipinnatus* 'Purity' (Asteraceae)
34. *Cleome spinosa*, spider flower (Capparaceae)
35. *Gaura lindheimeri* (Onagraceae)
36. *Zinnia* (Asteraceae)
37. *Salvia viridis* 'Blue' (Lamiaceae)

38. *Scabiosa atropurpurea* (Dipsacaceae)
39. *Aquilegia alpina* 'Hensol Harebell' (Ranunculaceae)
40. *Lathyrus* 'Cupani', sweet pea (Papilionaceae)
41. *Digitalis purpurea*, foxglove (Scrophulariaceae)
42. *Lunaria annua*, honesty (Brassicaceae)
43. *Smyrnium perfoliatum*, Alexanders (Apiaceae)
44. *Anethum graveolens*, dill (Apiaceae)
45. *Alchemilla mollis* 'Robustica', lady's mantle (Rosaceae)
46. *Chelidonium majus* 'Flore Pleno', greater celandine (Papaveraceae)
47. *Impatiens glandulifera*, Himalayan balsam (Balsaminaceae)
48. *Lobularia maritima*, sweet alyssum (Cruciferae)
49. *Lobelia erinus* (Campanulaceae)
50. *Asperula orientalis*, oriental woodruff (Rubiaceae)
51. *Anthriscus cerefolium*, chervil (Apiaceae)
52. *Petroselinum crispum*, parsley (Apiaceae)
53. *Satureja hortensis*, summer savory (Lamiaceae)
54. *Rumex acetosa*, sorrel (Polygonaceae)
55. *Levisticum officinale*, lovage (Boraginaceae)
56. *Borago officinalis*, borage (Boraginaceae)
57. *Lavandula spica* 'Hidcote Blue', lavender (Lamiaceae)
58. *Ocimum basilicum*, basil (Lamiaceae)
59. *Foeniculum vulgare* (bronze form), sweet fennel (Apiaceae)
60. *Myrrhis odorata*, sweet Cicely (Apiaceae)

61. *Agrostemma githago*, corncockle
    (Caryophyllaceae)
62. *Papaver rhoeas*, field poppy (Papaveraceae)
63. *Leucanthemum vulgare*, ox-eye daisy (Asteraceae)
64. Mixture of Annual Varieties
65. Mixture of Perennial Varieties
66. California Wildflower Mixture
67. *Lilium regale* (Liliaceae)
68. *Lilium formosanum* var. *pricei* (Liliaceae)
69. *Papaver rupifragum* (Papaveraceae)
70. *Papaver sendtneri* (Papaveraceae)
71. *Papaver somniferum* (Papaveraceae)
72. *Papaver nudicaule*, Iceland poppy (Papaveraceae)
73. *Meconopsis cambrica*, Welsh poppy
    (Papaveraceae)
74. *Argemone mexicana* (Papaveraceae)
75. *Argemone pleiacantha* (Papaveraceae)
76. *Ipomoea tricolor* 'Heavenly Blue'
    (Convolvulaceae)
77. *Tropaeolum peregrinum*, canary creeper
    (Tropaeolaceae)
78. *Tropaeolum ciliatum* (Tropaeolaceae)
79. *Eccremocarpus scaber*, glory flower
    (Bignoniaceae)
80. *Rhodochiton atrosanghineum* (Scrophulariaceae)
81. *Dicentra scandens* (Papaveraceae)
82. *Aconitum hemsleyanum* (Ranunculaceae)
83. *Lathyrus sativus* var. *azureus* (Papilionaceae)
84. Old-fashioned Sweet Peas, Mixed (Papiolionaceae)

the seed list

85. *Phaseolus coccineus*, scarlet runner bean (Papilionaceae)
86. *Lantana camara* (Verbenaceae)
87. *Thunbergia alata*, black-eyed Susan (Acanthaceae)
88. *Canna indica*, Indian shot (Cannaceae)
89. *Melianthus major* (Melianthaceae)
90. *Solanum quitoense*, naranjilla (Solanaceae)
91. *Solanum laciniatum*, poroporo or large kangaroo apple (Solanaceae)
92. *Ricinus communis*, castor oil plant (Euphorbiaceae)
93. *Mirabilis jalapa*, marvel of Peru (Nyctaginaceae)
94. *Rehmannia angulata*, Chinese foxglove (Scrophulariaceae)
95. *Isoplexis isabelliana* (Scrophulariaceae)
96. *Dianthus barbatus*, Sweet William *(Caryophyllaceae)*
97. *Dianthus deltoides* 'Flashing Light' or 'Leuchtfunk' (Caryophyllaceae)
98. *Arum italicum* var. *pictum* (Araceae)
99. *Eremurus robustus*, foxtail lily (Liliaceae)
100. *Gentiana asclepiadea*, willow gentian (Gentianaceae)